W9-AAW-489

GOOD ❖ OLD ❖ DAYS®
Live It Again™
1946

WILLIE GILLIS
Norman Rockwell

Dear Friends,

The year of the wedding—that's what 1946 was!

There were more weddings per capita in the United States of America in 1946 than any year in history. World War II had put thoughts of love and marriage on the back burner for millions of Americans, but the return of our victorious servicemen and women from the battlefields of Europe and the South Pacific brought romance back into focus almost immediately.

The end of the war crystallized the human need for love and family. Young men—many of them mere teenagers when called to national service—were matured beyond their years by the rigors of battle. Now they needed the comfort of home and hearth.

Some returned to sweethearts left behind at the beginning of the global conflict. They had tucked away frayed photographs in flak jackets and helmets long enough. Maybe they couldn't exactly pick up where they had left off, but their love found a way to bridge the chasm of four years and thousands of miles.

They had tucked away frayed photographs in flak jackets and helmets long enough.

Others brought back war brides—girls from England, France and other war zones—and a fresh wave of Old World culture swept through many American families.

The result, of course, was predictable. The record number of marriages in 1946 brought the first salvo of the Baby Boom. Life in America began to wend its way from the farm (and the inner city, for that matter) and toward suburbia. The seeds of modern American society were sown in those millions of marriages in the year of the wedding—1946.

©CORBIS © 1946 SEPS

Contents

MeadSchaeffer

Everyday Life

Winter vignettes

Winter brought a whole new world of togetherness to the neighborhood, especially for those who could find a hill for sledding. Often, entire families would gather with sleds, inner tubes and homemade gear designed for speeding down the hill. Sometimes, those sledding would use sheets of wax paper to help make sleds slicker for faster runs.

At the nearest pond, skaters would gather to frolic on the ice or to set up an energetic game of hockey, but not before a round of hard work shoveling snow off of the ice.

Of course, there was always the artistry of making snowmen and winter figures, often with a twinge of competitive spirit with the neighbors down the street.

Winter wasn't all fun, especially for those heading to work trudging through the fresh snowfall to brush the snow off their cars.

"We can't let on to that crowd, but I'd give anything to know where the highway is."

Life in the City

A day in town

The heartbeat of a nation coming back to life economically and socially especially could be sensed in the city with the screeching of streetcars, smells of street vendors and rush of the crowd to the downtown shopping district. Long lines formed at movie theaters, restaurants were full of patrons again, and department stores developed attractive facades and designs to beckon customers.

The rush of crowds on weekends was fueled by those who drove into the cities from surrounding rural areas to shop and take in the sites and sounds of city life. Family outings brought excitement about sidewalk popcorn and hot dog vendors, and a chance to eat out at the small corner "mom and pop" cafes.

After the end of the war, the population in cities began to grow steadily as new industries offered employment opportunities to city and rural residents.

Streetcars provided transportation for those working downtown. Many rode the cars for the novelty of it and for shopping excursions.

"Why, Mrs. Pemberton! I ain't seen you since we was slappin' tanks together at the war plant in '44."

Crowded sidewalks in the downtown shopping districts were a tell-tale sign of a nation beginning to prosper economically.

FAMOUS BIRTHDAYS

Diane Keaton, January 5
American actress

Naomi Judd, January 11
American country singer

The theater was a popular attraction for those visiting and living in the city. Productions often involved many people working behind the scenes to keep the plays running smoothly.

SILENCE
PLEASE
PLEASE
EN EL
TOREO
SILENCE
WIND THUNDER

Life in the City

After dark

The illumination of street and building lights gave the city a new flare of attraction for life after sunset. Stores were open until later in the evening, and industries began to run longer shifts.

The concept of "nightlife" became a fixture as an emerging time to socialize. Nightlife in the city included restaurants open until midnight, an increase in social events and a new way of living that made many rethink the concept of going to bed early and getting up at the crack of dawn.

LIBRARY OF CONGRESS, PRINTS AND PHOTOGRAPHS DIVISION, FSA 5A30763

Activity continued well after the clock struck 11 p.m. on city nights.

Attending formal evening activities became commonplace for those caught up in a new social world of evening meals, productions and nights "out on the town."

© 1946 SEPS

©GETTY IMAGES

The Metro Daily News

FINAL EDITION

JANUARY 10, 1946

THE UNITED NATIONS GENERAL ASSEMBLY OPENS

Its first session is in London.

Neatly designed streetscaping emerged to add attractiveness to downtown businesses and hotels.

Life in the City

Street scenes

Design and architecture became an important part of marketing city growth as the postwar economy began to improve and prosper. Downtown gardens and streetscaping coupled with various types of theme architecture added appeal to the business district.

Improved infrastructure provided for a more modern approach to restaurants, hotels and public buildings. The addition of swimming pools and new equipment to city parks provided new playtime opportunites for neighborhood children.

In addition, the sounds of housing construction could be heard as cities expanded.

Shops, restaurants and gift boutiques sprang up near train stations, bus depots and airports.

FAMOUS BIRTHDAYS

Dolly Parton, January 19
American country singer and actress

Gene Siskel, January 26
American film critic

"Okay, run in front of him—and good luck."

CIVIC OPERA
HOUSE
JOHN FALTER

Welcome Home

The journey back

The good news of the end of World War II left soldiers with a battery of emotions. Many returned home still in shock, anticipating the embraces of their loved ones, but still living in the framework of the survival techniques they had adapted to during the war.

Those coming in from the west gazed at the eastern horizon in search of the Golden Gate Bridge, exhilarated with its shadow as they sailed beneath its shelter. Others literally kissed the ground as they emerged from their ships at San Diego and other western points.

Those approaching New York Harbor wept with excitement as they saw the "Grand Old Lady" with her torch of freedom reaching high to welcome them home.

Above and beyond all else, the returning soldiers listened for the welcome cries of familiar voices they had longed to hear during months and years of service.

Others celebrated in jubilation with civilians as they arrived at depots across the country.

"At every stop he rushes out, shouts 'Darling' and kisses a dame"

Some servicemen arrived with somber faces, reflecting the world of terror and shock they had come from.

© 1946 SEPS

Many children spent every spare moment in the arms of their fathers who returned from World War II service. There were many stories and storybook reading sessions to catch up with.

Welcome Home

The soldiers return

Banners flew, confetti filled the air and signs welcoming home family members and boyfriends flowed from the masses as soldiers returned to American soil from service in World War II. Large signs with family names awaited many of those who had served as they stepped off trains and buses.

A nation that had sacrificed on the home front in order to generate supplies for the military was invigorated with the return of thousands that constituted family, a fresh workforce and the future of the nation's prosperity.

For many, personal embraces were filled with drama that had been communicated in letters and cards. In many cases, stories began to flow of military service while others buried the experiences deep in their souls and reached out to those they loved for healing and friendship.

© 1946 SEPS

"Pop, meet Captain Bixby and Colonel Johnson."

REPRINTED WITH PERMISSION FROM THE DR. PEPPER SNAPPLE GROUP

For many, arriving home was not only a return to family and loved ones, it was walking into the arms of fiancées and girlfriends who had waited patiently for the moment to continue with the dreams of life. Many of the military heroes were given near-celebrity status as they shared their stories with family, friends and neighbors.

The Metro Daily News FINAL EDITION

JANUARY 29, 1946

THE CENTRAL INTELLIGENCE GROUP FOUNDED

It is the predecessor to the CIA.

"Who, ME?"

Fitting back into civilian clothing was often a challenge to those returning from war. The image of the civilian self in the mirror was an adjustment. But for most, the change to civilian clothes brought hope for the future and the relief of being home.

"The major is having a hard time converting to a felt ha

Welcome Home

From uniforms to civvies

For those returning from the war, converting back to civilian life wasn't always as easy as it seemed. After living under strict rules in the face of constant danger, living in freedom and style took weeks and sometimes months of adjustment.

Some of the first concerns included finding a place in the civilian workforce, purchasing new clothes and relaxing back into everyday civilian living. Often, the change from uniforms to civilian clothing was symbolic of the end of fighting and the return to "normal" life. For those who had left family behind, adjusting into the home they returned to was often very challenging.

"You're a swell looking guy in civvies, too!"

Post War Anecdotes

For a period of time after the end of WWII, *The Saturday Evening Post* encouraged servicemen to share stories of the lighter side of their experiences in the military. They called these stories "Post War Anecdotes." Here are a few of our favorites from 1946.

The Sergeant Draws His Pay

A *POST* WAR ANECDOTE

I HAD been in the Pacific theater only a few months, but I was griping that day as I stood in the pay line. Due to various transfers, I had been red-lined—not paid—the two preceding months. "Boy, will I be glad to get this dough!" I said to a master sergeant in line ahead of me. "For a whole month, now, no smokes, no cokes, no nothin'. It's been tough."

"Be glad to get mine, too," the sergeant murmured. "It's been a long time."

The way he said it made me look at him more closely, and I saw how thin he was, with tired wrinkles in his young face and his hair turning gray. But I went rattling on, "So you've been red-lined, too, eh? Ain't it somethin'? Don't us Joes have enough trouble without this Army goofing off and making us wait for our dough?"

The line moved, and now he was in front of the pay window. I paid no special attention as the captain began counting out money to him. But instead of stopping after a while, the captain kept on and on. The stacks of bills piled up until it looked as though the sergeant was drawing pay for a platoon, not just one man. Afterward I found out that the amount was $8659.51, one of the largest pays ever drawn at one time by an enlisted man in World War II.

As he walked off with better than 17,000 pesos, I asked the soldier behind me if he knew who the sergeant was. The soldier said, "That's Master Sergeant David W. Clawson, of Lincoln, Nebraska. He's been in twenty-one years. He's drawing his back pay after thirty-seven months as a POW in Bilibid prison." I stopped griping.

—CPL. WARD B. STONE.

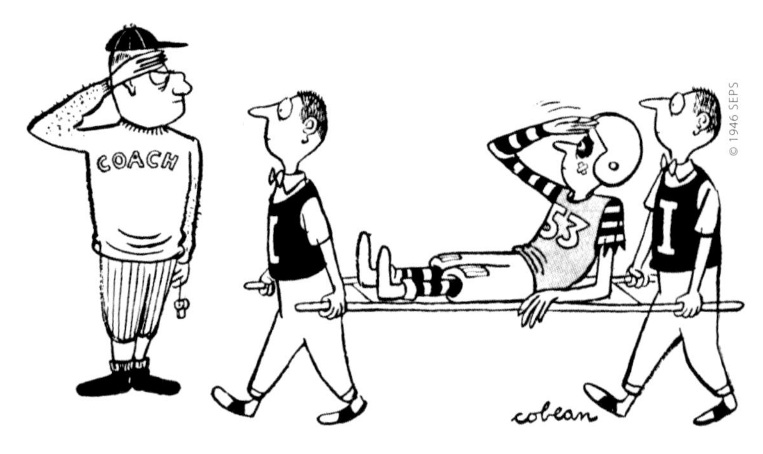

The 98-Yard Question

A *POST* PEACE ANECDOTE

THE problem of the returning veteran worries football coaches too. Bo McMillin, coach of Indiana's Big Ten champions, was afraid servicemen might not take kindly to discipline by a civilian. So he determined to make an example of Bob Hoernschmeyer, the first star to report.

On the opening play of scrimmage, Hoernschmeyer carried the ball through the whole first team, racing ninety-eight yards for a touchdown. Feeling that the star might be in need of a lesson in humility, Bo called him before the squad and lectured him on his faults. Just about everything he had done was wrong, according to Bo. Once he cut back too deeply, again he failed to cut sharply enough, his timing on straight-arming was off, and he had failed to give his blockers a chance to cover him.

"Now, do you have any questions?" Coach McMillin concluded.

"No, sir," said Hoernschmeyer, as he started for his position again. Then, pausing, he looked at McMillin and asked gravely, "How was it for distance, coach?"

—WALTER STEIGLEMAN.

So the Crew All Went Ashore

A POST WAR ANECDOTE

SOMETIMES it's hard to square our Navy regulations with common-sense dictates, as many a salty skipper will testify. I'll never forget how neatly a certain captain solved the problem one day when it became necessary to "splice the main brace"—that is, do a bit of celebrating by means of stimulating beverages.

His command, an assault transport carrying a full load of soldiers but a light cargo load, moved into Leyte Gulf during the invasion of Leyte Island in the Philippines. Over the side went the troops, and within three and a half hours the 450 tons of cargo were delivered to the beach, something of an unloading record for transports. As dusk fell, the ship shoved off for Kossal Passage in the Palaus, under orders to stay there until the gigantic Battle of Leyte Gulf, then obviously brewing, was over. A thin-skinned transport would be a sitting duck in a surface engagement.

When the radio flashed word of the great victory, the captain knew that under naval tradition it called for a celebration. There was canned beer in the holds—transporting beer is now allowed on Navy vessels—but regulations forbade drinking it on a Navy ship. And the only near-by land, Babelthuap Island, was still in Jap hands. So the captain did some rugged thinking, and pretty soon he came up with the answer.

When everything had been placed in readiness, he took the public-address microphone and said to the crew, "It is now time to splice the main brace to celebrate our victory. If you will go to the starboard gangway, you will find Elbow Island is on our beam. Each man will be issued two cans of beer at the quarter-deck. But he must go ashore on the island before he drinks it."

There was an island there, all right—a huge life raft which the captain had ordered prepared and put over the side by one of the booms.

—ROBERT G. PHIPPS.

She Saw Her Duty

A POST WAR ANECDOTE

THE train was typical of wartime urgency. Within the dimly lit coach a capacity crowd of servicemen and civilians slept fitfully against uncompromising seats while the Georgia countryside sped past the windows. Conspicuous in the confusion of strangely positioned forms was an elderly lady, a smile on her face as she sat serenely among a tangle of military arms and legs. Beside her a sergeant nodded; on the seat facing her sprawled two sleep-drugged privates.

As the train slowed down with a jarring lurch for a local stop and the disturbed passengers sleepily shifted their positions, a large shoeless foot unceremoniously deposited itself in the lady's lap. The foot's big toe was protruding from a gaping hole in the sock.

The sergeant awoke, saw the derelict foot, and looked with embarrassed concern at his elderly companion. But the lady was unperturbed. She regarded that bare toe calculatingly, then opened her purse and took out a needle, some brown cotton and a pair of scissors. Soon she was swiftly and deftly darning the damaged sock, working around the bare toe so skillfully that its owner went right on slumbering. When the task was done, she gently shifted the foot from her lap and put away her sewing things.

"Ma'am," whispered the sergeant, "how'd you ever do that without even waking the guy up? You deserve a medal."

The old lady smiled. "Oh, it isn't hard any more," she said. "That's the third G. I. sock I've mended on the hoof since the train started."

—T/SGT. DICK LESSERAUX.

G.I. Brides

Journey to America

After serving long stretches based in other countries, American G.I.s often interacted closely with the local population. Many service men married women they met during those war years. In some countries, especially liberated European countries, G.I.s were even looked upon as generous heroes who could offer new opportunities.

After the close of fighting, both G.I.s and G.I. brides struggled to make their way to America. Although there were war brides lucky enough to return with their new husbands or with the help of the U.S. Army, many more had to find their own way to America.

Reportedly, in the years 1942–1952, as many as 100,000 G.I. war brides came from the United Kingdom, while 150,000–200,000 came from countries in Continental Europe, and around 17,000 came from Australia and New Zealand.

Although not as common as marriages to women from Allied countries, there were also G.I. brides from Japan and Germany. These marriages were frowned upon, and the women were forced to follow more regulations than their fellow British and European G.I. brides.

The Metro Daily News

FINAL EDITION

FIVE CENTS

FEBRUARY 21, 1946

THE OFFICE OF ECONOMIC STABILIZATION REESTABLISHED

Truman attempts to control inflation.

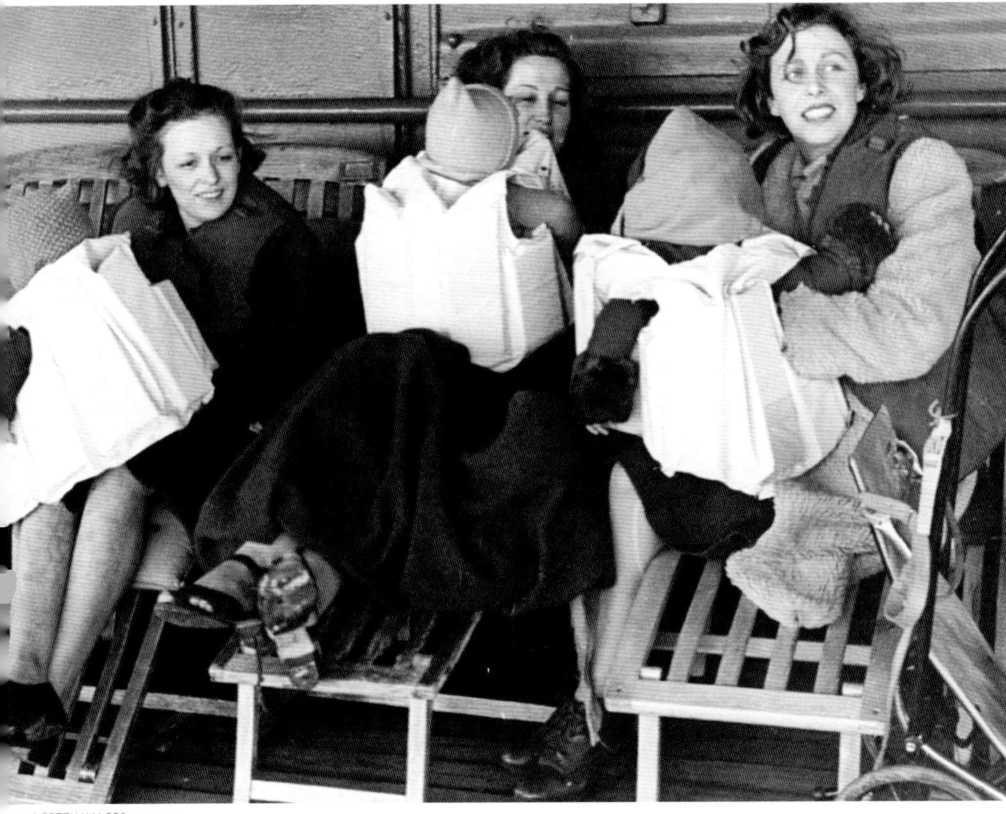

In many cases, like with these British G.I. Brides, wives already had children with their American husbands. Many wives had to wait months for permission to come to America while they were separated from their husbands, who had already made the journey back home to the States. While wives were anxious to join their husbands, they also had to face leaving their own ancestral families to be in a foreign land.

The United States Army started "Operation War Bride", which concentrated on bringing G.I. Brides to America. The first group of 455 women and 132 children landed in American on February 4, 1946. The Cunard White Star liner *Queen Mary*, a war ship especially commissioned to take war brides to America from the British coast, was one of the first to board on February 3. However, due to bad weather, the hundreds of G.I. brides aboard were delayed for their trip to America.

Everyday Life

Wedding bells

In churches across the country, bells tolled the news that the war was over and life was moving on. After years of waiting, many young couples planned their weddings as soon as the young men returned from service.

With the boom in marriages from all of the soldiers returning home after the war, even young girls began to dream of their own wedding days.

Weddings during the war often occurred in nice Sunday dress, minus formal wear. That all changed as the spirit of jubilation returned with soldiers and the end of the war.

FAMOUS BIRTHDAYS

Gregory Hines, February 14
American dancer and actor

Tyne Daly, February 21
American actress

Alan Rickman, February 21
English actor

During the war, many weddings were held in private ceremonies or in small parties, sometimes when soldiers were home on furlough. The return of military personnel to America brought back more extravagant weddings and celebrations.

What Made Us Laugh

"Too much salt in the potatoes again, dear?"

"Now whatever possessed me to get my arm caught in here?"

"Don't you think we've had our money's worth out of it yet?"

"Let's wait until one o'clock and all eat together."

"Well, if it won't write put it outside for the public to use."

"I'm afraid we'll have to let him soak overnight."

"You haven't by any chance quit bailing!"

"Shucks, I missed him!"

Travel the World

By air

With the war over, air travel expanded rapidly into areas that had been off limits. The freedom to fly into Europe once again brought a rush of intrigue for those curious to see famous world sites and visit cities that had been affected by the war. In addition, the phasing out of a high demand for war equipment allowed industries, including airplane manufacturing, to increase production once again.

Once the war was over, airport traffic increased almost immediately, with excited travelers putting on their Sunday best outfits to travel world wide. Young couples began to travel far for their honeymoons with family and friends seeing them off at the airport.

Tourist travel to such places as the Colosseum in Rome increased rapidly while nations such as Italy began to rebuild following World War II.

Travel to tourist spots such as Paris flourished almost overnight once the war ended in the European theater. Major cities in Europe readily embraced tourists as postwar life took on new meaning and tourism could bring much needed money into the recovering cities.

The Metro Daily News

FINAL EDITION

FEBRUARY 24, 1946

COL. JUAN PERÓN WINS ELECTION AS PRESIDENT OF ARGENTINA

With help from his wife, Evita, he rules until 1955.

The Metro Daily News

FINAL EDITION

MARCH 5, 1946

CHURCHILL DELIVERS "IRON CURTAIN" SPEECH

He touches on the Cold War during talk at Westminster College.

Travel the World

By sea

The year 1946 was a breakout year in passenger sea travel. After the war ended, safe waters welcomed thousands of ship liners carrying passengers to all parts of the world. Many of the original ships had been withdrawn from service to become troop ships. Once the war was over, they were reconditioned and returned to civilian service.

One of the best-known passenger liners returned for civilian use was the *Queen Elizabeth*, one of the largest passenger liners ever built. The spacious ship, built in 1938, was used as a troop transport ship during the war, and then returned to commercial use in 1946. Veterans who had served in the war would sometimes return to their troop ship with family members to enjoy its service in more pleasant times.

Travel Will Be Fun Again
via Canadian Pacific

Remember how pleasant it used to be to travel on Canadian Pacific ships! Remember the cuisine, the courteous service, the fun of shipboard life . . . and the ships themselves!

Just now there's a big job to do repairing the wear and tear of wartime years—replacing lost ships . . . but, when it's done, travel will be fun again — the Canadian Pacific way!

Soon a new, two ocean fleet will plow the sea routes of the world . . . and once again it will be possible to go from Shanghai to Southampton — Canadian Pacific all the way!

Canadian Pacific

SPANS THE WORLD

JOHN
FALTER

Exploring America

In the city

As traveling opportunities began to expand, Americans spent more time visiting cities they had always heard or read about, but had never seen. Many took family vacations to New York City to see the Statue of Liberty, Empire State Building, Central Park, Radio City Music Hall and Fifth Avenue.

Others traveled to metropolitan areas such as Philadelphia, to see the early government buildings, Los Angeles, to see the surrounding movie production studios, and Chicago, for shopping excursions at Lake Michigan storefronts. Historical cities, such as Boston, also drew many tourists fascinated with the early New England heritage.

Train and bus stations became some of the busiest metropolitan areas as tourists from around the country began to explore growing cities.

Passenger trains arriving in large city depots became a welcome sight to those relatives and friends receiving loved ones, and to local merchants cashing in on the tourism industry.

Everyday Life

The concert

Learning to play musical instruments was very popular in a world where entertainment was still simple and often centered around at-home performances.

In some instances, several members of one family possessed musical talent in playing various instruments. It was not unusual for families and neighbors to gather in the evening or on Sunday afternoons in each other's homes to enjoy a neighborhood orchestra or special recital.

On warm summer evenings, surrounding neighbors could benefit from the musical tones drifting through open windows and screen doors.

Musical recitals in homes provided evening and weekend entertainment for the neighbors, family and friends of the musician involved. Classical music was particularly popular for the more formal presentations.

"Okay, son—now comes the commercial!"

Homes would sometimes pack out for recitals or neighborhood concerts. Sometimes a featured singer or musician would be brought in for a special party.

The Metro Daily News

FINAL EDITION

FIVE CENTS

MARCH 5, 1946

OPPENHEIMER RECEIVES MEDAL OF MERIT

He is recognized by President Truman for his work on the Manhattan project.

Musical Fun

"All right, dear; she's asleep now."

"I always said that boy had talent."

"I don't suppose it's very good for the clarinet, but it's the only way we can get him to practice."

"Well, what do you remember from last week?"

MARCH #7
ARCH #7
ARCH #7
Stevan Dohanos

Fun on the Water

Fishing

"Personally, I don't consider Atkins a sportsman."

"The last ones were half spaghetti."

Aspiring fishermen had their own ideas about which gear and tackle was most effective for their desired fishing catches. The use of rods and reels became more popular, as opposed to using the old cane pole, especially in fishing rivers and small ponds.

FAMOUS BIRTHDAYS

Liza Minnelli, March 12
American singer and actress

Timothy Dalton, March 21
Welsh actor

Dedicated fisherman endured all types of weather in order to catch proof of their successful fishing excursions.

Fun on the Water

Sailing

As postwar society began to prosper, those wealthy individuals living near water began to invest in sailboats, yachts and other expensive water equipment. Spending a day at sea to fish or simply relax became a common way to get away from the riggers of working.

In addition to boats, many began to invest in lakeside properties and cottages, not only along major bodies of water, but along smaller inland lakes where the concept of "going to the lake for the weekend" became popular. It became a great way for families to spend time together. For some, sailing for sport also became a popular pastime.

"Okay, Miss O'Neil, you can lean on this side now."

Taking a picnic lunch and spending an entire day on the lake became a good way to relax and catch up on some visiting. There was something about dropping anchor beneath a strong breeze and warm sun that was attractively mesmerizing.

4E 483
4E 483
BLESSED EVENT
C Atherton

Stevan Dohanos

Baseball

America's pastime

Just as America was welcoming its returning soldiers in 1946, the sporting world saw a return of war veterans and baseball heroes. Baseball had continued to be played across the country during World War II, but the end of the war brought back many baseball legends to the game. Ted Williams was discharged early in 1946 and later that same year he was awarded the MVP of the American League and was a major player in the World Series for the Boston Red Sox, who lost by a close margin to the St. Louis Cardinals. Stan Musial, the MVP of the National League and the Sporting News Player of the Year, returned that year from a short stint in the Navy. Many major league players finished out the year maintaining their status as heroes in baseball, but were recognized as war heroes as well.

Bob Feller, shown here signing autographs on April 30 after his second no-hitter, was also a Navy veteran who returned from the war just the year before. Feller was the earliest major league player to enlist—on December 8, 1941—immediately following the attack on Pearl Harbor.

Joe DiMaggio, (shown with his arm around brother, Dom, at left) a war veteran who served with the U.S. Army Air Forces, played in an American League all-star game against Dom's team, the Boston Red Sox. DiMaggio had to face the embarrassment of borrowing a Red Sox uniform from his brother as his own Yankees uniform did not arrive in time for the game.

NARA, COURTESY OF UNITED STATES HOLOCAUST MEMORIAL MUSEUM PHOTO ARCHIVES

Karl Brandt, shown above, was Hitler's personal assistant and Reich Commisser for Health and Sanitation and was held responsible for many of the horrible experiments performed in concentration camps. He, along with Hermann Goering, shown below, were considered especially guilty of crimes against humanity and received death sentences. Goering was Hitler's designated successor and commander of the *Luftwaffe*.

NARA, COURTESY OF UNITED STATES HOLOCAUST MEMORIAL MUSEUM PHOTO ARCHIVES

The Nuremberg Trials

War criminals brought to justice

NARA, TRUMAN LIBRARY

Although the Trials had begun the year before, 1946 saw a great deal of the more infamous Trial of the Major War Criminals (24 of the most prominent leaders of Nazi Germany) before the International Military Tribunal. There had been long preparation and talks between allied leaders Roosevelt, Churchill and Stalin over how to deal with war criminals. By 1945, the IMT had been appointed with a group comprised of judges and prosecuters from a variety of allied countries. The trials were to take place at the Palace of Justice, one of the few buildings left standing in Nuremberg. The trials took place over many months with the prosecution taking from Nov. 20, 1945, to March 6, 1946, to state their case and interview witnesses. The defense rested at the end of June after allowing all remaining 21 Nazi leaders (the other three were either dead or too frail) to give their testimonies. Verdicts were handed out on Oct. 1.

The Metro Daily News

FINAL EDITION

APRIL 1, 1946

TSUNAMI STRIKES BIG ISLAND OF HAWAII

More than 100 are killed and thousands injured.

NARA

In the front bench, four of Germany's most notorious Nazi leaders await questioning. From left to right sit Hermann Goering, Rudolf Hess, Joachim von Ribbentrop and Wilhelm Keitel. Each received a guilty verdict of either death by hanging or life imprisonment.

Post War Anecdotes

Prayer for Two

A *POST* WAR ANECDOTE

PETE was a lanky, droll Tennessean, and the best runner—message bearer—a platoon leader ever had.

One day he stood peering over the edge of our foxhole into the gloom of Germany's Hürtgen Forest, disdaining to duck as jerry mortar shells were thumping down all around us.

"Pete," I asked him, "don't you suppose the good Lord gets a little tired hearing us pray over and over, 'Please, Lord, pull me through this one and I'll never ask it again,' and then, fifteen minutes later, coming right back with the same line?"

"Yep, I reckon He does, lieutenant," drawled Pete. "But I don't always pray for myself. Sometimes I pray for you."

"You do!" I exclaimed, touched by this show of sentiment.

"I sure do," Pete said. "Bein' your runner—wal, a good deal of the time I'm standin' pretty damn close to you."—ARNOLD C. SHAW.

Penny Had a Phrase for It

A *POST* WAR ANECDOTE

DURING these war years, Penny and I have been trying to live alone and like it as best we can, with daddy far away and so many problems to solve all by ourselves. The main one of these has been to make our allotment s-t-r-e-t-c-h to cover rent and food and clothes and doctors and dentists and War Bonds! When these are all taken care of, there is nothing to speak of left, and so we have had to devise fun that doesn't cost anything. That's where our window-shopping came in! We soon discovered that one can enjoy everything in the world there is to see in every kind of store, so long as one is content with just looking. This wasn't easy at first, but finally we became regular window-shopping addicts, and derived an amazing amount of satisfaction and pleasure from this harmless pastime.

But one day our good intentions backfired on us while we were doing a particularly extensive job of both windows and interior of a big five-and-ten-cent store. We were lingering perhaps overlong at one of the counters, fascinated by its colorful display, and were finally approached by a salesgirl, who asked us pleasantly if she could help us.

Imagine her astonishment and consternation, to say nothing of mine, when Penny, her lesson well learned, fixed the girl with a wide, blue-eyed gaze and assured her earnestly, "Oh, no, thank you! We're just shoplifting!"

—MARION KNOPF.

The Perfect Comeback

A *POST* WAR ANECDOTE

THE English girl who served as cashier in the junior officers' mess at 8 South Audley Street in London never seemed to see any humor in the typical American wisecracks of the Yank pilots who engaged her in conversation. She considered these young men a brash lot. She was annoyed by their invitations to come to their flats for a drink, and she was especially irritated when one would archly remark, as if offering irresistible bait, that he had silk stockings.

She must have given the situation some thought, because one day she brushed off an annoyer with memorable neatness and dispatch. A good-looking young pilot strolled up, and the conversation went like this:

PILOT: "What are you doing tonight?"

CASHIER: "Oh, nothing special."

PILOT: "Why not come over to my place for a drink?" Then, leaning nearer, "I have silk stockings."

CASHIER: "Really? I have too. But tell me," she said in a confidential voice, "how do you keep yours up?"

Exit pilot, limping.

—J. A. MCCARTHY.

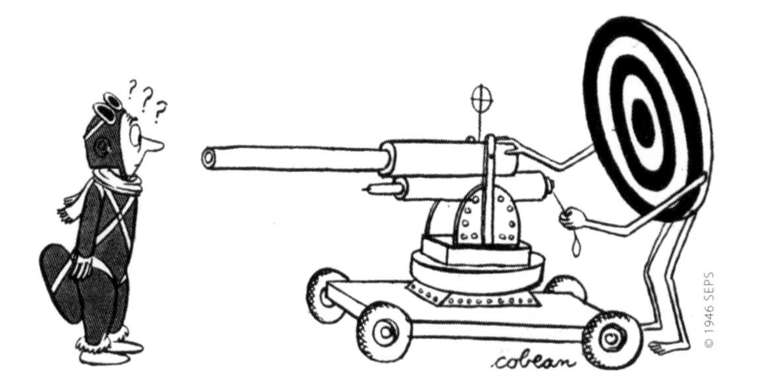

One Man Had a Question

A *POST* WAR ANECDOTE

ON this cold, bleak morning in mid-November of 1944, we waddled up to the briefing tent in our overstuffed flying clothes with the premonition that today something out of the ordinary was going to take place. Sure enough, an unusual sight greeted our eyes. The over-all briefing map of the battle zones was covered!

The intelligence officer slowly stepped forward and, amid the rattle of maps, dropping of equipment, chronic coughing and ever-present whispering of briefing tents, he announced, "Gentlemen, today your target is Schweinfurt, Germany. You will go in at twelve thousand feet."

I remembered that in the disastrous Schweinfurt raid in 1943 our big brothers, the Forts, had gone in at twice that height and still lost more than 600 men. I was plenty scared. I barely heard the intelligence officer say, "There will be a hundred seventy-five guns to the right of your course, two hundred and twenty-five guns to the left of your course, and over the target you will be within range of two hundred and eighty guns for three to five minutes."

An ominous hush had come over the pilots, bombardiers, navigators, gunners and the "ever-faithfuls"—the guys that were going to sweat us out. In the whole assembly I could detect neither sound nor movement. Even the little clouds of white smoke a person makes when exhaling on a cold morning were absent. Life was standing still and the future hung in the balance.

With the stereotype finish for briefing, the group commander stepped forward and asked: "Gentlemen, are there any questions?" Then it came. From somewhere in the assembly of warriors, a meek voice chirped up, "Sir, is this trip really necessary?"

—PAUL E. MULRENIN, 1ST LT. AC.

The Last Straw

A *POST* WAR ANECDOTE

DURING my two and a half years overseas I heard many a soldier gripe about the hardship, the food, the pay and the officers. But the most eloquent beef I ever heard was at Atlantic City, when I had been in the Army a little more than a week.

The day's schedule for us recruits began with an address by an officer on the importance of buying lots of War Bonds and of making a regular pay-roll allotment for that purpose.

Then we marched four miles to the drill field and paraded up and down until eleven o'clock, when we began our weary trek back to our hotel for chow.

Not yet accustomed to this mode of existence, we were probably dragging along rather listlessly—too much so for the taste of our robust drill sergeant.

"What will all these civilians think of you?" he cried heartily. "Let's sing in cadence, and keep it up all the way in!"

This was the last straw to the man who was puffing along beside me. Anything but the outdoor type, he had to use all his will power to keep his chin off the ground.

"Listen to the man," he gasped. "First they want us to fight the war, then they talk us into financing it . . . and now he's asking us to entertain the civilians."

—THOMAS B. LOGUE

Boots in a Fog

A *POST* WAR ANECDOTE

IN the days when our amphibious force was in training and making its old-Navy tutors weep in their grog, one of the first LST's was delivered for a shakedown cruise on Chesapeake Bay. When the ship was returning to Hampton Roads on the last day of the trial run, a fog came up and, according to custom, the executive officer—second in command—took his station in the bow while the captain remained on the bridge, high in the after part of the ship.

The exec, who in peacetime was a young Tennessee lawyer just out of the farming country, had never been out in a fog before, and he didn't like it at all. When he had peered for a while into the awful nothingness which kept rushing toward him, he grabbed the intraship telephone and suggested plaintively, "Hey, captain, it's getting darn foggy up here! Hadn't we better anchor?"

The skipper just mumbled something derisive about landlubbing lawyers, and hung up.

The LST went plowing on, the void got thicker and thicker, and presently the exec was on the phone again—this time with more urgency in his voice. "Listen," he said, "I can't see my hand in front of my face out here! How the devil much longer is it going to be before that anchor goes down?"

By now the captain was really annoyed. "Look, you inland sailor," he roared over the line, "I don't want to hear one more peep out of you, you understand? You just run your end of this thing and I'll run mine!"

For about ten more minutes the telephone was silent while the fog took on the density of something that shouldn't happen anywhere but London. Then suddenly there was an explosive clatter of chains up forward and the exec was on the skipper's telephone again.

"Captain," he announced brightly, "I don't know what you're doing with your end of this boat, but I just anchored mine."

—LIEUT. J. R. GREGORY, USNR.

U.S. DEPARTMENT OF ENERGY

Nuclear bomb testing, which would take place between 1946 and 1958 on the Bikini Atoll, began with "Operation Crossroads." The Baker explosion, shown above, took place on July 25, 1946. The wide-spanning cloud surrounding the center shows the "Wilson chamber effect," a condensation cloud. A tall geyser of water formed in the center, which fell back into the lagoon. Some of the ships docked nearby were contaminated by the highly radioactive water released by the explosion.

Atomic Energy

Postwar development

After the dramatic, tragic and yet successful results of the use of atomic energy at the close of World War II, President Truman looked to find more beneficial and progressive uses of its power. Congress continued to look to atomic energy for nuclear weapons for defense, but also as a way of maintaining world peace, promoting public welfare and creating more employment and enterprise opportunities by way of a nuclear industry. This new look at atomic energy included large-scale experiments on the Bikini Atoll in the Pacific Ocean starting in July 1946.

UNITED STATES NAVY

A fleet of U.S. Navy F6F-5K Hellcat drones await their trip across the cloud formation above Bikini Atoll in order to test radioactivity. The planes were marked with numbers and colors dependant on their particular radio guidance frequencies.

NARA, TRUMAN LIBRARY

On Aug. 1, 1946, Truman signed the Atomic Energy Act (also known as the McMahon Act). This Act was to start the move of the production of nuclear energy and operations of the Manhattan Project over to the newly formed Atomic Energy Commission. This transfer, which took place on Jan. 1, 1947, meant that there would be far more civilian control over nuclear technology and information, as opposed to it being a strictly military entity. The Act was to be radically altered by the Atomic Energy Act of 1954.

Improved modes of production were adapted from making war materials to making products for peacetime needs.

Industry

America's economic engine

The emergence of the World War II industry ended the continuing effects of the Great Depression and created a bridge to economic prosperity following the conclusion of the war. By the mid-1940s, American industry had been revitalized with sectors of it, such as defense production, evolving into aerospace, and an emerging new concept, atomic energy.

Other war-induced benefits included the strengthening of organized labor and a technological resurgence that created an atmosphere of expectation among scientists, engineers, government officials and private citizens.

Americans began to anticipate increases in personal income and quality of life; that, in itself, led to diligence and research in the industrial revolution following the war.

The steel industry that had become prosperous in war manufacturing returned its efforts to automotive and other heavy industrial production.

FAMOUS BIRTHDAYS

Ed O'Neill, April 12 American actor

Tim Curry, April 19 British actor, vocalist and composer

As production increased, organized labor sought to improve working conditions for heavy industrial labor.

The agricultural industry was greatly enhanced by the increased transportation of grain through the train industry.

New ways and means of feeding industrial demands became essential in the face of increased business prosperity.

Industry

The faces of progress

Industry that had become successful during World War II began looking for ways to expand its success to benefit the postwar economy. The massive research and development during the war had greatly impacted the scientific community. Along with the return of a large amount of workforce potential from those who were in war service, new levels of technology began to lead the nation into new forms of industry.

The oil industry, which had fueled planes and army vehicles, continued to expand its development to serve a growing automotive revolution. As industrial advances were made, the need for new machinery and parts grew with the times.

Mead Schaeffer

Many strikers organized across different cities. Above, Meyer Stern, a C.I.O. District leader, speaks to a mass meeting of meat packing plant workers. Not only did masses of workers walk out of plants in New York to demand higher wages, but also in Chicago and other cities. Meat packing plant leaders feared a stop to the nation's meat supply.

Labor Unrest

As soldiers returned from fighting, the job market went into upheaval despite the improving economic environment. Veterans fought to get their jobs back, as well as fair wages for the scarce jobs available. Many veterans felt that a job was owed to them after they had spent years sacrificing and endangering themselves to fight for their country. On the other end, older workers had to fight to keep their jobs with the new surge of younger workers.

It seemed like no industry or city was untouched as strikers arose from meat packing plants, electric companies, steel factories and even schools and other non-industrial business. From New York to Chicago to Detroit, labor unrest became prevalent throughout the country.

©CORBIS

©CORBIS

These members of the Foremen's Association are protesting steel and auto plants gradually "easing out" older workers.

©CORBIS

Not even the world of high fashion was untouched by labor unrest in 1946. These professional models take a break to reapply make-up while protesting the replacement of cover girl models with "folksy art" on the covers of *Coronet* magazine.

Women worked in large numbers for bigger companies. Often young women got their starts in the workforce by training as secretaries or typists.

Everyday Life

White collar America

While men were away at war, women stepped into jobs, including management positions, vacated by those serving in the military. However, when soldiers returned from the war, social norms implied that women should step aside and give the jobs back to the men.

Some women were willing to do that, but weren't so inclined to step down for the male world. While the male gender still ruled white collar America, perceptions of feminine roles were beginning to change drastically.

Intermingled with all of this was the role of returning veterans to the workforce. Creating jobs for them was a challenge. While many returned to former positions, others were forced to retrain for new jobs because of changes in their work places while they were gone.

Pictures of men and women working together often reflected the implied roles of the time, with men shown behind the desk with women approaching from the front of the desk.

The Metro Daily News
FINAL EDITION

May 7, 1946

TOKYO TELECOMMUNICATIONS ENGINEERING FOUNDED

It is the predecessor to Sony.

"Jammnerphs Muschkvlopt and Cphompany—Dear Shir:"

When veterans returned to the workforce, they had to adjust to dealing with a different type of stress than they did during the war.

FAMOUS BIRTHDAYS

Candice Bergen, May 9 American actress

Robert Jarvik, May 11 American physicist and artificial heart inventor

Everyday Life

Young families

When soldiers returned from World War II, many of them married the girlfriends they had left behind. Others became engaged to those they had developed a special correspondence with during the war.

Out of the postwar marriages emerged the beginning of the "baby boomer" generation, with children being born into a world beginning to prosper with economic success and the return of family warmth and happiness.

REPRINTED WITH PERMISSION FROM HART SCHAFFNER & MARX

Family life brought healing and happiness to homes that had been saddened by distance and concern during the war.

The "baby boom" after the war meant that many returning soldiers had to learn quickly how to be fathers.

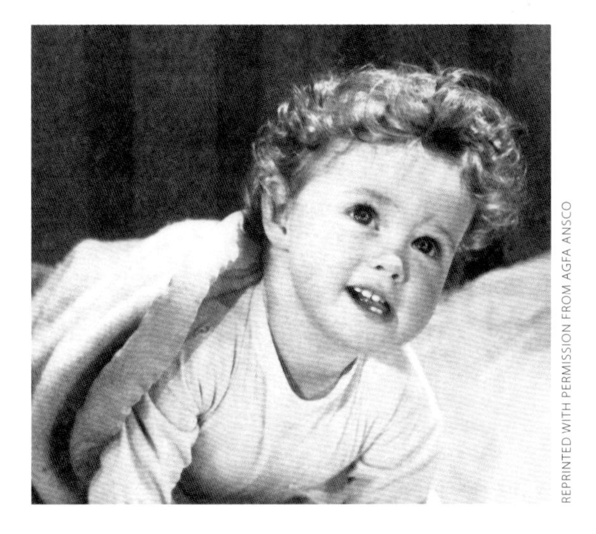

REPRINTED WITH PERMISSION FROM AGFA ANSCO

School Days

Globes were popular as hands-on tools for those seeking to visualize the lessons of geography class.

"Here's my report card and one of yours I found in the attic."

Memorization and class recitation were major parts of learning in the 1940s. "The Midnight Ride of Paul Revere" and portions of Shakespearean plays were popular choices among English teachers of the day for students to memorize for class presentations.

FAMOUS BIRTHDAYS

Reggie Jackson, May 18 American baseball player

Cher, May 20 American actress and singer

G. Brook

5 SEPS

Good Morning, Children!
Stevan Dohanos

School Days

The country school

Many of Norman Rockwell's paintings of rural life include scenes in and around the old country school. Children walking through snowdrifts, carrying dinner buckets, bundled in scarves and mittens was a common scene along country roads during good or bad weather.

Chalk and slates were primary teaching tools, while teachers also found yardsticks to be beneficial for teaching more than learning at times. Students were often seated according to class, with girls on one side of the school and boys on the other.

In addition to school time, the country school was often used for spelling bees, Christmas and Easter programs and occasionally for various types of community forums.

Often in a small, rural town, the entire school could be photographed together in one picture.

Students would gather around the teacher as she read a story to the entire class, minus the student who wanted to read her own story. During winter months, students would gather together just as closely to the old pot-bellied stove that heated the school.

© 1946 SEPS

Everyday Life

On the ranch

Ranch life on the range lands of the Great Plains and the great open country of the western states was still rather primitive and filled with daily challenges. Many ranchers were still coming into their own following the great Dust Bowl days of the mid-1930s.

During the summer months, roaming the ranch and caring for cattle and horses often became a father-son connecting point. But the presence of buffalo herds and severe weather elements still challenged ranch life at every turn. Still, the competition of rodeos and enjoyment of evening "hoedowns" added spice to the hard work.

LIBRARY OF CONGRESS, PRINTS AND PHOTOGRAPHS DIVISION, FSAC 1A35021

The Metro Daily News

FINAL EDITION

MAY 21, 1946

KLM FLIES BETWEEN AMSTERDAM AND NEW YORK

It is the first European airline to have scheduled flights across the Atlantic.

OHN FALTER

A fishing expedition to the nearest river or lake was often accompanied by a cookout a campout and sometimes a sleepover. Walking sticks were popular during journeys down a nearby trail.

Everyday Life

Boys' adventures

A boy could satisfy his curiosity along a river bank with a fishing pole, up in a tree or running to greet the mailman with the family dog by his side. Those who lived close to a railroad made their way toward the train at the sound of a whistle to wave to the engineer or passengers on board.

Cowboy hats and accessories were particularly popular with young boys and led to neighborhood re-enactments of radio show favorites. For many, involvement in Boy Scouts helped solve the need for adventure, while neighborhood clubs also provided an outlet for creative endeavors.

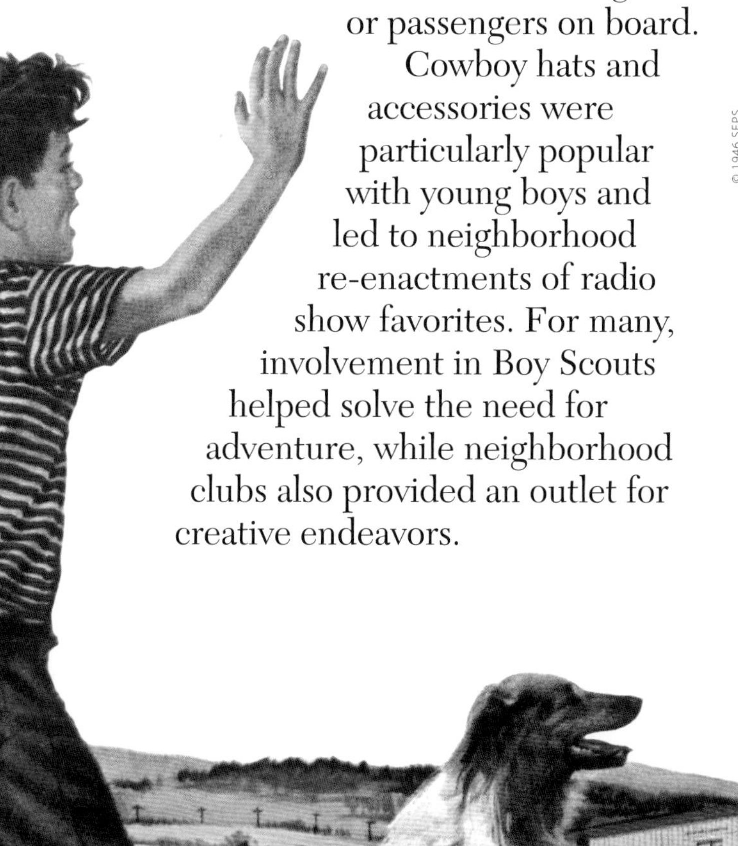

A boy's best friend, the family dog, was usually not far away when he set out looking for some adventure.

"Well, I would run away, only I'm not allowed out of the block."

Everyday Life

Man's best friend

Young puppies enjoy bringing gifts to their family; selected items would range from the fireman's hat to toys, socks and other potential "gifts" within view.

"He's a smart dog—you can't teach him a thing.

Bathing and grooming the family pet meant getting out the wash pan and cleaning accessories for what often proved to be a major family chore.

A best friend puppy was always a welcome companion in a moment of reflection.

NO DOGS
ALLOWED
Mgr. Super Market
23¢

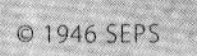

Everyday Life

The games kids play

Andy Over, Red Rover, Red Rover, and Hopscotch were just a few of the games that were popular around one-room schoolyards during recess. On May 1, there was always the colorful wrapping of the May Pole tradition. Of course, games such as baseball, basketball and hockey were also very popular.

During the summer, those games were taken from recess to backyard gatherings in the neighborhood. Some games such as Hide and Seek and Kick the Can demanded a bit more creativity, while other games evolved at the ornery whims of energetic youth.

Active participation in playing outside demanded a lot of energy, and sometimes, at the right time, mothers would provide an opportunity for a break with such snacks as homemade donuts, cookies, brownies and milk.

"I notice there was plenty of dust on her closet shelves."

What Made Us Laugh

"I can't promise that I can go to the movies, Teddy—but I have pretty swell parents."

"Here, Frankie—see if Beethoven's Fifth fits any better."

"That smile and attitude mean only one thing—he wants a volunteer for something!"

"Nothing—I already knew how to stand in the corner."

"Didn't it strike you the author repeats himself in Pat-a-Cake, Pat-a-Cake, Baker's Man?"

"We finally caught him for you, lady— but he gave us quite a chase."

"What happened to the six guys who were in between?"

"It contains my personal effects. Why?"

Just like today, most students had many nights of studying for long hours.

Everyday Life

College life

Norman Rockwell's conclusive painting of "Willie Gillis in College" depicts a relaxed Gillis, home from the war and finally settling into life with a future and purpose. Rockwell had brought his fictional character, Gillis, from his entry into the war until the college setting where he is depicted as being at ease and seemingly happy in the pleasant environment.

For many who had returned from service, the opportunity to attend college, and in some cases, finish high school and then attend college, gave a real psychological boost after the perils of war.

Even though attending college meant leaving home, for many families, having children a short distance away at college was much more preferable than overseas in the dangers of harm's way.

The 1946 college look still included wearing a tie in some instances, but guys wore looser coats as they sought to impress girls during study times together.

The Metro Daily News

FINAL EDITION

MAY 25, 1946

SWITZERLAND REPAYS STOLEN GOLD

The Swiss government agrees to repay $58 million in gold that was stolen from Jews by the Nazis and deposited in Swiss accounts during the war.

they're Sleek
they're Slim
they're Trim
they're Terrific!
Waterman's
Hear Gang Busters Saturday night, 9:00 E. T., 8:00 C. T., 7:00 M. T., 9:00 P. T.—ABC

REPRINTED WITH PERMISSION FROM YAFA AND THE CONKLIN PEN COMPANIES

REPRINTED WITH PERMISSION FROM THE SANFORD CORPORATION

Everyday Life

The art of writing

Good penmanship was considered to be an indication of personal pride and respect, both on the part of those writing and to those for whom the document or letter was written. Taking care to write legibly, good spelling, and good grammar were important skills to have when filling out job applications, making official signatures and writing to others.

For many, the success of good writing was based on purchasing good ink pens, those that would be easy to handle, but deliver a professional look with each stroke. In addition to writing done in the business world, many wrote pages a day in personal letters and journaling efforts.

REPRINTED WITH PERMISSION FROM THE SANFORD CORPORA

Measurably-"51" is the world's most wanted pe

Carter's Stylewriter

CHINESE RED

EBONY

Streamlined Beauty
Mechanical Perfection

Carter's newest and finest writing set $3.00

• In tune with 1946, Carter's Stylewriter is completely modern — engineered from gleaming plastic in seven rich tones. There's a Stylewriter to blend with every decorative scheme . . . in office, school, or home.

Entirely new in mechanical design, Stylewriter's exclusive expansion chamber prevents overflow from internal air expansion in warm rooms . . . and guards against spilling.

Stylewriter is equipped with a feather-light pen . . . balanced for easy writing . . . comb-fed to write a page or more at a dip. Easy to use, easy to fill, the ink reservoir is the standard Carter's Cube . . . available at stationery counters everywhere.

Stylewriter
for balanced writing... with Carter's balanced ink

The Carter's Ink Company, Boston, Massachusetts

Smooth-flowing for effortless writing, Carter's Ink is non-corrosive . . . the safest ink you can use for fountain pens . . . steel pens . . . or your handsome Stylewriter writing set. Carter's Ink comes in 9 rich colors . . . one for every personality.

Carter's *Balanced* **Ink**
starts fast – dries fast
helps pens last

MAHOGANY

IVORY

EMERALD

MAPLE

COBALT BLUE

Those wishing to have good clean writing would spend more to purchase ink pens that flowed freely, didn't create a mess and gave a nice artistic look to the print.

Looking Sharp

Dapper men

Following the war, men generally preferred clothing different from uniforms and without many restrictions. Suits were generously cut in pinstripe, herringbone or glen plaid fabrics. Men began to dress more casually with short sleeves becoming more common as street wear.

A trip to the local barbershop meant receiving a haircut with a slicked-back look without sideburns, exposing the man's full ear. Vests were discarded from suit-wear in favor of a more casual, looser fit.

Suits were tailored and pants were generously pleated and cuffed, with deep patch pockets.

"Where is my other garter?"

Robes and full-cut trousers were a sign of opulence and luxury, and were often worn as lounge wear.

The Metro Daily News

FINAL EDITION

JUNE 3, 1946

THE U.S. SUPREME COURT RULES VIRGINIA'S JIM CROW LAW UNCONSTITUTIONAL

There can no longer be segregation on buses.

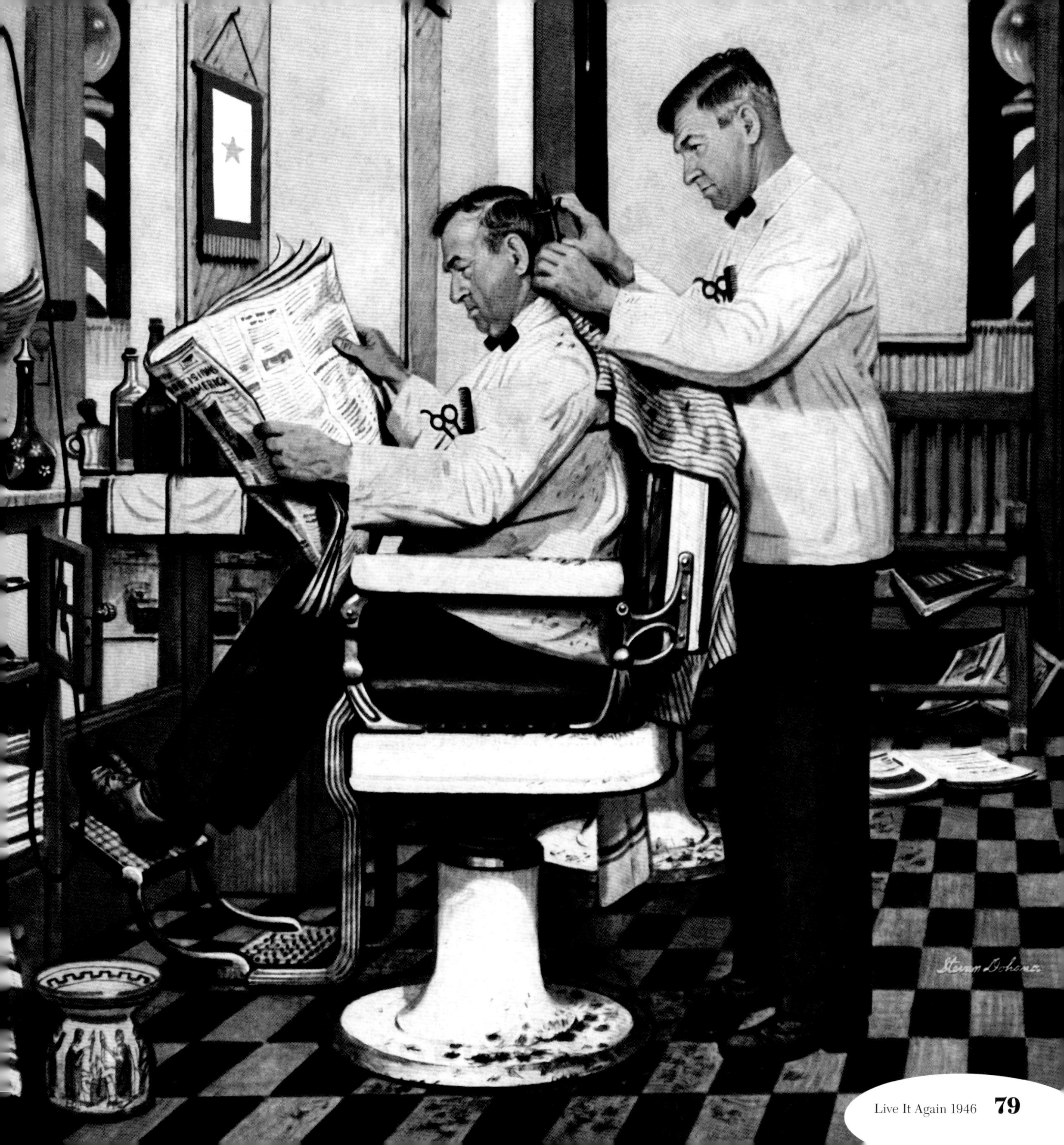

COURTESY OF THE DOW CHEMICAL COMPANY

A young lady could dream of a night out on the town as she held up a dressy, long gown.

LIBRARY OF CONGRESS, PRINTS AND PHOTOGRAPHS DIVISION, PPMSCA (

Consideration to trends and flattering lines was eve important when choosing clothes for active pursuit Young ladies were expected to wear fashionable sportswear, like this tennis outfit.

"Wait till you see this one!"

Looking Sharp

Ladies' fashion

Ladies' fashions in the "swing era" were still subject to some material conservation from the war, but there was also an indication of a loosening up to fuller dresses and gowns.

Ladies began to feel the freedom to purchase more clothes with a variety of classy styles; a growing economy and higher-paying jobs supplied more money for the purchase of clothes. More wrap-around dresses started to appear, an indication of a willingness to spend more money on dress material.

Hats, shoes and purses were still an important part of dressing well in 1946. Although sportswear became more prevalent after the war, having a put-together outfit was still important.

©GETTY IMAGES

Flowered hats and extravagant headwear were popular for formal events and those wanting to be noticed in public.

COURTESY OF THE DOW CHEMICAL COMPANY

The Metro Daily News FINAL EDITION

June 4, 1946
NATIONAL SCHOOL LUNCH ACT
President Truman signs the Act into law.

Looking Sharp

Dressing up

During the war, so many chemicals and other resources were used that cosmetics had become scarce. Within a short time after the war, dressing up became fashionable, including using various types of makeup.

Solid-colored evening gowns of the mid-1940s replaced the long flowered gowns of the pre-war era in the 1930s.

"Miriam, dear, you can't go outside with nothing on but mother's play suit!"

During the day, dresses were often a little more casual, natural and flowing.

Flower-studded hats and matching gloves were thought of as a "high concept look" of self-confidence.

Everyday Life

Just you and me

Dress wear was a bit more casual in 1946, especially for non-formal dates, with women wearing short-sleeve dresses and men wearing light coats.

Couples often enjoyed each other's company while dining at home during a night in.

Couples rolled up their pants legs and enjoyed spending time alone at the lake or some resort.

Couples were often grateful just to be together after a long separation due to the war.

alajálov
EGGS

Everyday Life

Home cookin'

Improvements in kitchen appliances made it possible to store food more effectively. The changeover from gas to electric range stoves introduced the possibility of new dishes and a new style of cooking.

While men worked, women who stayed at home baked goodies for the family and prepared a home-cooked dinner for all to enjoy as they gathered around the evening table to visit at the end of a day filled with hard work.

Gender roles started to change as men began assisting in the kitchen, cooking dishes that had normally been served by the women.

Your Great New
Frigidaire Cold-Wall
is Here

REPRINTED WITH PERMISSION FROM GENERAL MOTORS COMPANY

The coming of the electric range stove allowed for new oven dishes such as various casseroles and meat dishes.

© 1946 SEPS

The Metro Daily News

FINAL EDITION

JULY 1, 1946

BRITISH TRANSATLANTIC PASSENGER AIR SERVICE TO NORTH AMERICA BEGINS

Scheduled flying time between London and New York is 19 hours, 45 minutes.

Everyday Life

Home decor

Wood paneling, wall-to-wall carpeting, which was often patterned, and upholstered furniture were all part of the were all part of the evolving home decor in the mid 1940s.

Music filled homes as 78 rpm records played from solid oak record cabinets with hinged lid features. Many of the living room furniture pieces had low restful arms and backs and reversible cushions. Porcelain top tables made it handy for kitchen work and cleaning.

Home decor started becoming more simple with cleaner, more modern designs to go along with the emerging simpler lifestyle of the times.

Upholstered seats made chairs more comfortable; arms were often upholstered on the "master chair."

FAMOUS BIRTHDAYS
George W. Bush, July 6 43rd president of the United States
Sylvester Stallone, July 6 American actor
Cheech Marin, July 13 American actor and comedian

Preparing the home for dinner guests often meant arranging a showy dining room with opulent furniture and a generous view.

Maple bedroom furniture was considered one of the homey looks of the day. Famous furniture makers, like Mengel, used maple for their bedroom suites.

For Sale Fun

"If you're handy with a hammer, that could be made very cozy."

"And another feature is the excellent drainage."

"I can see it now. The cardboard walls—the corrugated-iron flooring—the celluloid windows."

"Of course, the $35,000 they're asking for it gives you the privilege of using the ocean."

FAMOUS BIRTHDAYS

Linda Ronstadt, July 15 American singer and songwriter

Danny Glover, July 22 American actor

"Remember! This is positively the last time I'm going to pretend you're the boss!"

"Okay—now when I give the signal, we all start yelling insults at Whittly—"

Everyday Life

The local shop

Small community shops were a source of upplies, medicine, groceries and treats for the local ıeighborhoods. From seeds and gardening tools to ;roceries, fresh fruit and meats, the local shops carried ·nough of a variety of goods that residents sometimes isited the establishments several times a day to ›urchase immediate needs.

For children, of course, a trip to the local shop with Λother always meant at least an attempt to get some ype of treat. Everything from cinnamon balls to suckers ould be found behind the counter at the cash register.

In addition, the small center served as a place to ocialize and catch up with the latest news around the ıeighborhood.

hildren often found many reasons why they deserved suckers, candy ars or other types of goodies.

While Father visited the store owner, a curious son spent much of his time discovering small toys and play things to purchase.

Everyday Life

The local diner

The local diner proved to be one of the most popular social places in the neighborhood. Residents who lived nearby would gather for coffee and a grill-prepared breakfast on the way to work. Those who were retired would often stop to grab a newspaper from the stand in front of the eatery, and then venture inside to catch up on the latest news of the community.

Cooks and waitresses got to know customers on a first-name basis, and for those with a pattern to their orders, food would be on the grill before they reached their seats. Quite often, there were three sets of crowds, one at each mealtime, and some patrons who stopped in for a mid-morning or late-afternoon cup of coffee.

In addition to home-cooking, diners were especially well-known for their large sweet rolls, cake and large selection of pie flavors.

Diners provided social settings to have a good visit or heart to heart chat over a cup of coffee and piece of pie.

"Better have one of the boys show that little Phillips fellow how to operate those mixers."

A visit to the diner by local law enforcement always provided a great source of the latest information to pass on to regular customers gathered around the counter for coffee.

Fresh fruit or sweets often sat beside an old-fashioned cash register as a final temptation for a purchase while customers paid before leaving.

Diner cooks often knew the problems of many who would chat with them at the counter over a daily cup of coffee.

The Metro Daily News

FINAL EDITION

July 25, 1946

DEAN MARTIN AND JERRY LEWIS STAGE FIRST SHOW AS COMEDY TEAM

LIBRARY OF CONGRESS, PRINTS AND PHOTOGRAPHS DIVISION, CPH 3C13825

Everyday Life

The soda shop

In the 1940s, soda fountains were gathering places for teens, family treats and a quick thirst quencher on a hot summer day. Nearly every drugstore had one; often those accompanying parents to the pharmacy would grab a quick Green River, Red River or Suicide soda while medicine was being dispensed to parents.

The local soda fountain also served as a great place to meet after school, or for a quick chat over various flavored sodas, sundaes, phosphates and flavored colas. Sometimes, parents would take their children to the corner fountain for a reward after completing a task. Downtown business people would find a refreshing break in the middle of the afternoon.

"Doesn't take long to run through a couple bucks, does it?"

D-Luscious
ICE CREAM
Special VIENNA ROAST 41¢
FRANKS AND BEANS 23¢
HOT TURKEY 51¢
JOHN FALTER

Young people in the communities learned how to work because they enjoyed assisting with projects involving adults that they looked up to.

Everyday Life

Small town community

The spirit of camaraderie in small town communities often resembled the lives of those families living in the town. Indeed, many in the town were closely related to other residents, and those that weren't were treated as though they were.

Each knew the concerns of the other, and when there were crises, community members assisted according to the need, whether it was help with work, providing meals or monetary assistance. Each helped mend the other's fences, each helped look after the other's children and no one was too busy for a visit at the local soda fountain or filling station.

The local church was the heart of the community. When the church bells rang, most people were either in church or on their way there. Communities poured unreserved energy into their youth, whether it was by attending a local school activity, or supporting fund-raising efforts for camp, scouts or other youth-oriented activities.

Waiting for ice cream at the local food stand provided a good opportunity to catch up with the happenings in the life of a neighbor.

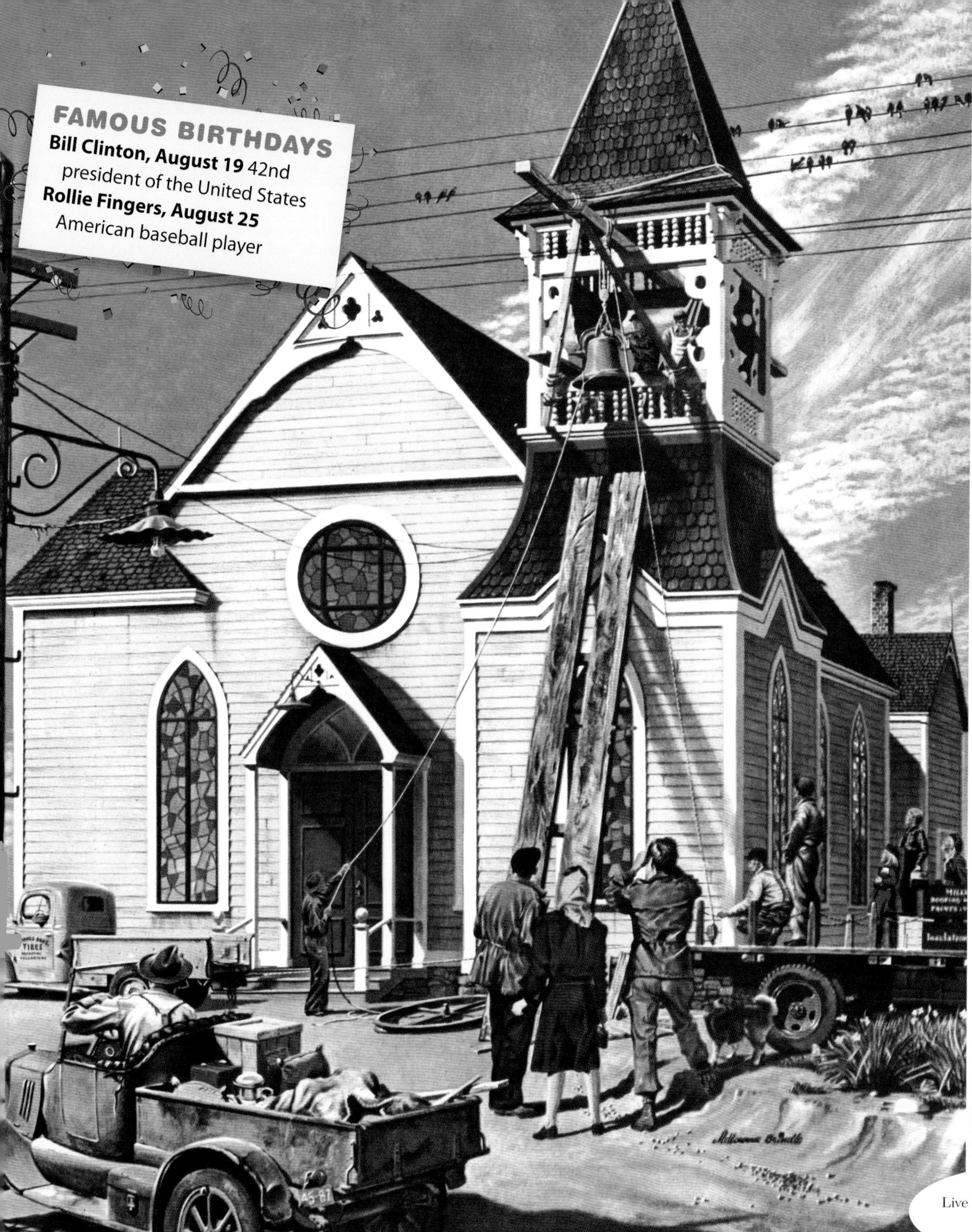

FAMOUS BIRTHDAYS
Bill Clinton, August 19 42nd president of the United States
Rollie Fingers, August 25 American baseball player

When work was needed on public buildings such as the church, able-bodied residents showed up to donate time and labor to see that things were taken care of.

© 1946 SEPS

The mailman knew those in his route personally. He always had time for a short friendly greeting. He was also willing to lend his hand in cases of need or an emergency.

Everyday Life

Around the neighborhood

A sense of tranquility and new appreciation for friends settled into neighborhoods with the return of military personnel from World War II. There was a sense of concern about assisting those returning and settling back into the community.

In nice weather, neighbors would often take time to be outside. Many residents would enjoy their neighborhoods by taking a walk around their streets or visiting a nearby park. Evening was often a time of visiting with others on the front porch or front steps during a stroll around the block.

FAMOUS BIRTHDAYS

Barry Gibb, September 1 British/Australian rock musician of the Bee Gees

Freddie Mercury, September 5 English singer of Queen

COURTESY OF THE DOW CHEMICAL COMPANY

Many neighbors took time to catch up on the week's activities following worship at the neighborhood church. Sometimes they would carry that spirit of friendship to each other's homes for Sunday lunch.

Local delivery men would sometimes find time for a friendly break with a cup of coffee and piece of pie at the neighborhood café.

Those who had been separated by miles during the war couldn't spend enough time together. Corner benches provided a good place for a quick visit and greetings from those passing by.

Special moments were made more personal by deliverers who took the time to hand deliver goods to the front door.

Everyday Life

Kids on the move

For kids, expanded travel opportunities opened up entire new worlds. The opportunity to fly, ride a train or go on a cruise provided a chance to learn about new destinations, and the experience of traveling in general.

Young people had the opportunity to become acquainted with relatives who lived at a distance and to see places they had only previously read about in geography class and magazines.

The sound of the train on the tracks often lulled young riders to sleep. Taking a nap also provided eager hearts with a sense of arriving sooner.

FAMOUS BIRTHDAYS

Tommy Lee Jones, September 15 American actor

Oliver Stone, September 15 American film director

Travel experiences allowed young learners to follow their movements to new destinations on maps.

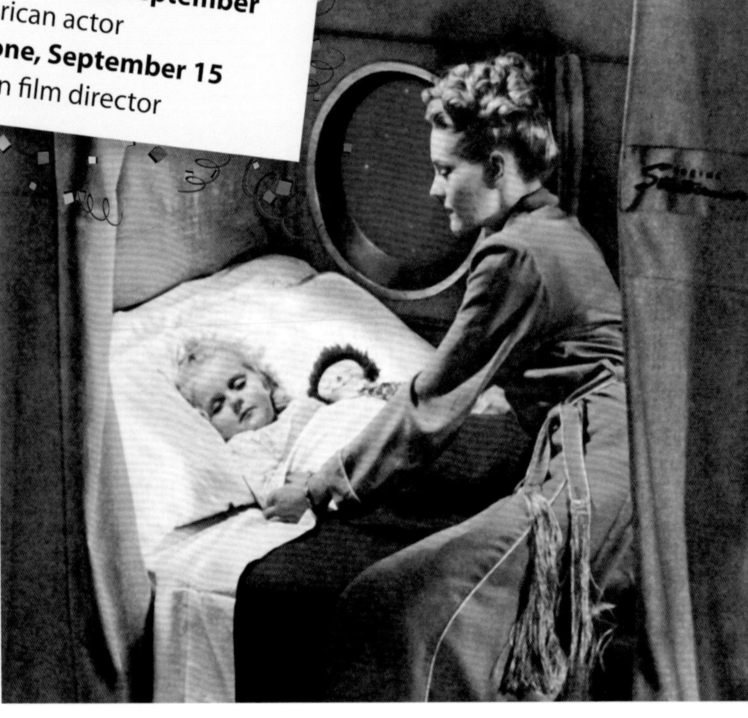

Sleeping on a strange bed while flying on a plane was still "home" as long as a favorite doll or stuffed animal was close by.

Trains were popular for transportation, especially due to their reputation for providing comfort and a speedy way to travel.

Trains

America's fascination

By the mid-1940s, passenger trains had become a real fascination for Americans, from both the standpoints of riding and observing. At the first sound of the train whistle, children and adults alike would run to windows or platforms to wave at passengers looking out the windows of arriving or departing trains.

Riding the train, complete with its own diner and pullman cars, had become an adventure for those traveling on family vacations and business trips. Many times, families would ride short distances just to experience a train ride.

Of course, there was also the excitement of military personnel coming back to their hometowns to community-wide celebrations.

The Metro Daily News

FINAL EDITION

OCTOBER 2, 1946

SMOKING SCRUTINIZED

The health hazards of smoking discussed at a medical symposium held at the University of Buffalo.

Many people took the train for the commute to work or between a small town and a nearby city for a day of shopping or running errands.

CRESTWOOD
norman rockwell

Memorable Cars of 1946

With the production of cars on the move once again, competitive selling points centered around appearance and new features such as exterior wood panels. Cars were being produced with easier-to-read instrument panels and steering wheel columns with new horn-blowing rings and center ornaments. Plymouth advertised a new starter button on the instrument panel that was considered to be especially appreciated by the ladies. Convertibles were also becoming more popular.

Since this was the first opportunity to purchase new cars since 1942, the demand was initially much greater than the supply.

Chrysler came out with new wood-panel siding on its "Town and Country" model.

Studebaker took on a sporty look for its "Champion" model.

The popularity of convertibles, like this De Soto, was on the rise.

Lincoln's "Continental Cabrio

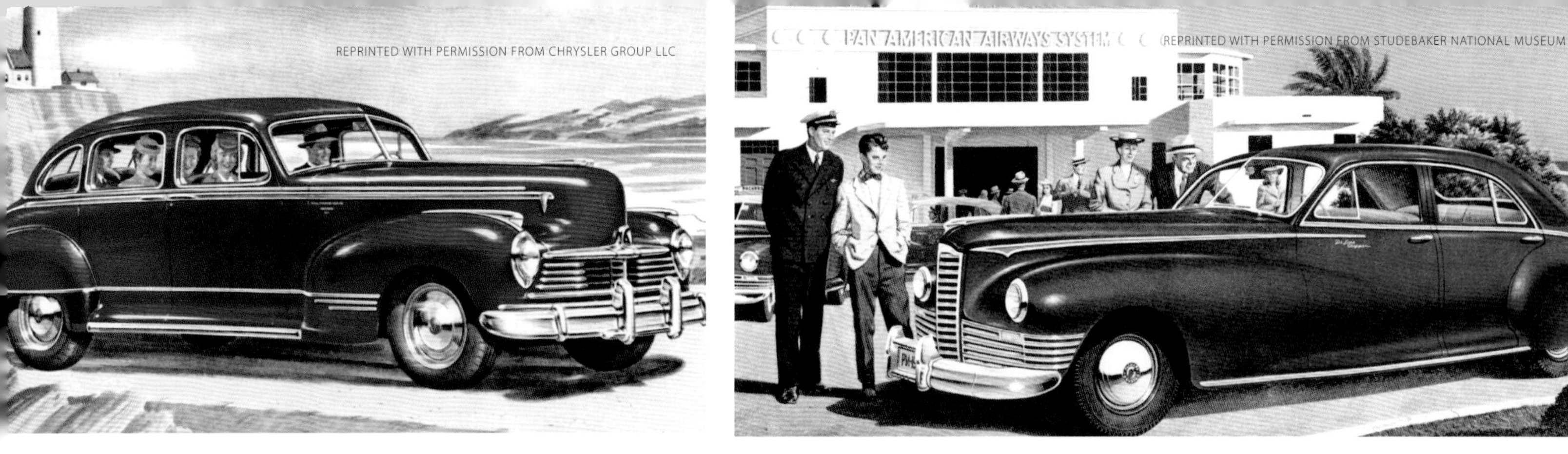

Buyers had a choice of a "super-six" or "super-eight" engine in Hudson's "Commodore" model.

Packard considered its "Clipper" model to be "America's #1 glamour car."

Kaiser and Frazer automobiles were introduced together in front of the Waldorf-Astoria Hotel in New York City.

Postwar Cadillacs incorporated the ideas of General Motors styling chief Harley J. Earl to become one of the most sought after style of cars on the market.

What Made Us Laugh

"Remember me, Professor Boggs? I sat 3rd from the end in the 2nd row and had a habit of asking rather impish questions."

"It's me, Dr. Hellin—I hope I didn't startle you."

"As nearly as I can understand your mumbling, madam, one of our office-supply clerks was rude—is that it?"

"I guess he isn't very mad."

"No, I won't take one. I'll not encourage your cat to be socially irresponsible."

"I've never seen him smile."

"Come on, Spike. Forget the small change."

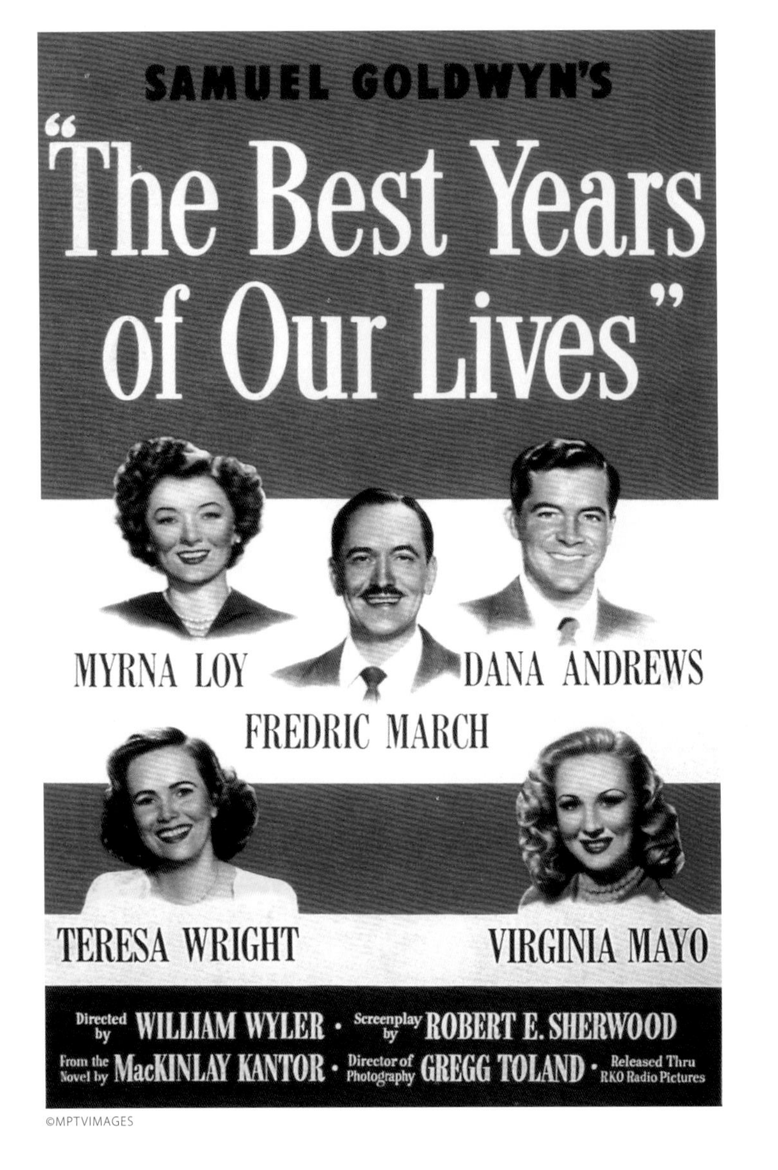

SAMUEL GOLDWYN'S
"The Best Years of Our Lives"
MYRNA LOY
FREDRIC MARCH
DANA ANDREWS
TERESA WRIGHT
VIRGINIA MAYO
Directed by WILLIAM WYLER · Screenplay by ROBERT E. SHERWOOD
From the Novel by MacKINLAY KANTOR · Director of Photography GREGG TOLAND · Released Thru RKO Radio Pictures

At the Movies

In 1946, the silver screen was a little less heavy with war films and had a variety more similar to pre-war Hollywood. Mysterious film noir was still popular with movies like *The Big Sleep* and *Notorious*. Dramas were abundant, but few comedies from the year made a lasting impression outside of the musical *Blue Skies*.

But more than any else, the end of World War II ushered in iconic movies reflecting both the joy of the end of fighting and the difficulties of returning to life as normal. *It's a Wonderful Life* encourages the optimism of postwar America, celebrating love, family and home. *The Best Years of Our Lives*, in contrast, paints a portrait of the struggles of the women and children who were left at home during the war and the returning veterans haunted by war. The importance of family and home is still central to the film, but its realism bars a too sentimental look at a recovering nation. The film won an Academy Award for Best Picture.

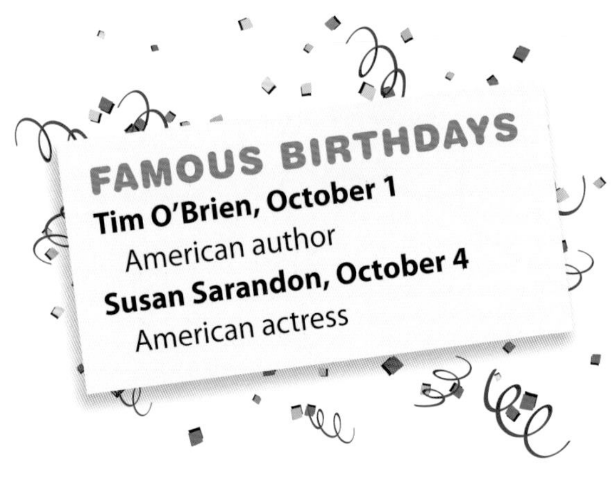

FAMOUS BIRTHDAYS
Tim O'Brien, October 1
American author
Susan Sarandon, October 4
American actress

It's a Wonderful Life was nominated for five Academy Awards, but failed to win any. However, director Frank Capra's film has been proclaimed by the American Film Institute as one of the 100 best American films ever made. The film is, perhaps, stars Jimmy Stewart and Donna Reed's most cherished film today.

At the Movies

Tops at the Box Office

- The Best Years of Our Lives
- The Big Sleep
- Blue Skies
- Duel in the Sun
- Gilda
- It's a Wonderful Life
- The Jolson Story
- Notorious
- The Postman Always Rings Twice
- The Razor's Edge
- The Yearling
- To Each His Own

In *The Big Sleep*, an adaptation of Raymond Chandler's novel, Humphrey Bogart plays the famous private detective Phillip Marlowe. Bogart's co-star was also his wife, Lauren Bacall. Bacall's agent, trying to combat negative press that Bacall received from the film *Confidential Agent*, asked that the chemistry between Bacall and Bogart be played up in *The Big Sleep*. Producers agreed and new scenes with more highly charged sexual dialogue were added.

FAMOUS BIRTHDAYS

Laura Bush, November 4 former First Lady of the United States

Sally Field, November 6 American actress

ılfred Hitchcock's thriller/love story *Notorious* ɔrings together a suave government agent ı the form of Cary Grant and a German ·xpatriate, Ingrid Bergman, recruited to ıfiltrate a group of Nazi Germans in hiding fter World War II. After filming, Grant kept the rop key for the wine cellar that was the set ɔr many prominent scenes in the film. After a ɛw years, Grant passed the key on to Bergman. Vhen Hitchcock was awarded the American ilm Institute's Lifetime Achievement award in 979, Bergman presented Hitchcock with the rop key, to his amusement.

The film *Gilda* is infamous for portraying Rita Hayworth as the ultimate femme fatale. The film makes several appearances in 1994's *Shawshank Redemption*. The famous introductory shot of Gilda popping her head into the frame is shown as the inmates have a movie night. The main character, Andy, also covers up the beginnings of his escape tunnel with a famous poster of Hayworth.

Johnny Mercer, shown here singing, had a big hit in 1946 singing the catchy "Personality." He also did a recording of the classic "A Fine Romance" with Martha Tilton. While Mercer had many successes with his singing, it was really his lyrics that brought him the most fame. Mercer won an Academy Award for Best Song for "On the Atchison, Topeka and the Santa Fe" for the film *The Harvey Girls*, released in 1946. Mercer also won the Award again in 1961 for his lyrics for the song "Moon River," used in the film *Breakfast at Tiffany's*

FAMOUS BIRTHDAYS

Gianni Versace, December 2
Italian fashion designer

Patty Duke, December 14
American actress

The Metro Daily News FINAL EDITION

DECEMBER 7, 1946

FIRE IN ATLANTA'S WINECOFF HOTEL KILLS 119

Music

1946 was a year of variety in the music world. Standbys like Frank Sinatra, Dinah Shore and Nat King Cole held on to their popularity, but some new voices began to be heard over the airwaves. B.B. King and Chet Atkins were starting their professional careers. Modern composer Igor Stravinsky premiered his *Symphony in Three Movements*. Famous Philadelphia Orchestra conductor Eugene Ormandy premiered Béla Bartók's *Piano Concerto No. 3*. Broadway shows *Annie Get Your Gun* and *Show Boat* saw a surge in popularity.

Top Hits of 1946

"Personality"
Johnny Mercer

"(I Love You) For Sentimental Reasons"
Nat King Cole

"Prisoner of Love"
Perry Como

"Let it Snow! Let it Snow! Let it Snow!"
Vaughn Monroe

"To Each His Own" The Ink Spots

"Five Minutes More" Frank Sinatra

"McNamara's Band"
Bing Crosby

"Choo Choo Ch'Boogie"
Louis Jordan & His Tympany Five

"The Gypsy"
Dinah Shore

Perry Como, shown at left, topped the charts in 1946 with hits "Surrender" and "Prisoner of Love." Three years before, Como signed with RCA Victor and stayed with the record company for the rest of his career. Como had success in many areas of entertainment, including radio, theater, nightclubs and television. Como's distinctive, personable and humble style won over many fans.

"Now we'll hear the other side."

REPRINTED WITH PERMISSION FROM AMERICAN AIRLINES, INC.

Everyday Life

Small town Christmas

Celebrating Christmas in small towns was all about heritage and traditions. Toy stores and dime stores were open late into the evening to allow residents to purchase gifts for the community's children. Most trees were hand-cut and many of the ornaments were homemade.

After gathering at the local church for the Christmas program, many families would reunite back home to enjoy a home-cooked meal. Often neighbors and friends would get together to celebrate by listening to music, sharing goodies and enjoying a warm fire.

REPRINTED WITH PERMISSION FROM SPARTON CORPORATION

Men often visited along the street while their wives stood in line to purchase gifts for children and family members.

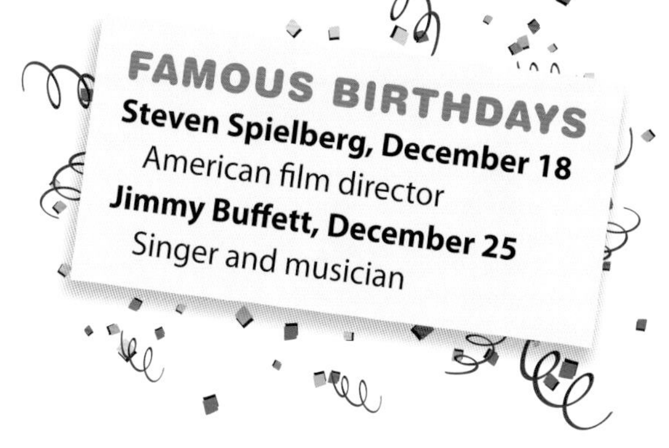

FAMOUS BIRTHDAYS
Steven Spielberg, December 18
American film director
Jimmy Buffett, December 25
Singer and musician

A freshly fallen blanket of snow provided a white Christmas and a bright spot in the long winter darkness.

The Metro Daily News

FINAL EDITION

DECEMBER 26, 1946

105-ROOM FLAMINGO HOTEL AND CASINO OPENS ON LAS VEGAS STRIP

Everyday Life

Winter fun

A good snowfall brought lots of winter fun to energetic children, right in their own backyards. Quite often, the entire family would get involved in making snowmen, with creativity contributing to the alternative look of many snowy critters.

For the neighborhood gang, it was a good time to settle a few things with snowball battles at the local forts and other imaginary standoff creations.

On Main Street, there would be the hustle and bustle of those coming to town to shop and catch up on the latest news following a few days of life stuck at home due to a winter storm.

Sometimes the adventures of winter days stretched beyond safety, but a soft blanket of snow and the helping hand of a good friend cushioned any unexpected falls.

More *The Saturday Evening Post* Covers

The Saturday Evening Post covers were works of art, many illustrated by famous artists of the time, including Norman Rockwell. Most of the 1946 covers have been incorporated within the previous pages of this book; the few that were not are presented on the following pages for your enjoyment.

THE SATURDAY EVENING
POST
MARCH 9, 1946
10¢
TELEVISION:
Boom or Bubble?
By ALVA JOHNSTON
SALT LAKE CITY
By GEORGE SESSIONS PERRY
THE SATURDAY EVENING
POST
JUNE 8, 1946
10¢
BEGINNING:
EISENHOWER'S SIX
GREAT DECISIONS
By
Lt. Gen. WALTER (Beetle) SMITH
General Ike's Chief of Staff
Tells the Fascinating Inside
Story of How We Beat Hitler
A Complete Novelette
By ROBERT RICHARDS
THE SATURDAY EVENING
POST
APRIL 6, 1946
10¢
THE PLAYBILL

THE SATURDAY EVENING
POST
JULY 6, 1946
10¢
Double Treasure
By CLARENCE BUDINGTON KELLAND
The Book-of-the-Month Club
By PETE MARTIN
POST
10¢
We're Teaching the Children to Lead Japan
By HAROLD J. NOBLE
THE BLACK MARKET BROKE US
By CELIA FARVISH
THE SATURDAY EVENING
POST
AUGUST 3, 1946
10¢
THE GREAT PENICILLIN MYSTERY
By STEVEN M. SPENCER
PITTSBURGH
By GEORGE SESSIONS PERRY
THE SATURDAY EVENING
POST
SEPTEMBER 14, 1946
10¢
A Complete Novelette
By WILLIAM E. BARRETT
PHILADELPHIA
By GEORGE SESSIONS PERRY

THE SATURDAY EVENING
POST
SEPTEMBER 21, 1946
10¢
PIGSKIN PREVIEW
By FRANCIS WALLACE
Beginning:
The Battered Bride
By ROBERT CARSON
THE SATURDAY EVENING
POST
SEPTEMBER 28, 1946
10¢
MR. BIG NOSE BRINGS
HOME BRITAIN'S BACON
By EDGAR SNOW
Also . . .
A Complete Murder Mystery
By ROY HUGGINS
POST
DECEMBER 7, 1946
10¢
ST. LOUIS
By JACK ALEXANDER
A Complete Novelette
By NELIA GARDNER WHITE
Norman Rockwell
THE SATURDAY EVENING
POST
OCTOBER 26, 1946
10¢
WHAT'S WRONG WITH
AMERICAN MOTHERS?
By DR. EDWARD A. STRECKER
Atlantic Graveyard
By LESLIE ROBERTS

January 3
John Paul Jones, English rock bassist of Led Zeppelin

January 6
Syd Barrett, English rock guitarist and singer of Pink Floyd

January 8
Stanton Peele, American psychologist
Robby Krieger, American rock musician of The Doors

January 20
David Lynch, American film director

January 21
Johnny Oates, American baseball player and manager

January 24
Michael Ontkean, Canadian actor

January 27
Nedra Talley, American singer of the Ronettes

February 2
Blake Clark, American actor and comedian

February 5
Charlotte Rampling, British actress

February 9
Séan Neeson, Northern Irish politician

February 19
Karen Silkwood, American activist

February 20
Brenda Blethyn, English actress

February 28
Robin Cook, British politician

March 4
Michael Ashcroft, English entrepreneur

March 6
David Gilmour, English rock musician of Pink Floyd

March 7
Peter Wolf, American rock musician of the J. Geils Band

March 15
Bobby Bonds, American baseball player and manager

March 26
Johnny Crawford, American child actor and musician

April 7
Léon Krier, Luxembourgian architect

April 16
Margot Adler, American journalist

April 20
Julien Poulin, Canadian actor

April 25
Talia Shire, American actress
Strobe Talbott, American journalist

May 4
Harvey Goldsmith, British impresario

May 7
Thelma Houston, American singer

May 10
Donovan Leitch, Scottish rock musician

May 16
Robert Fripp, British musician

May 19
André the Giant, French professional wrestler

May 22
George Best, Northern Irish footballer

May 26
Mick Ronson, English guitarist

June 18
Russell Ash, British author

June 23
Ted Shackelford, American actor

June 24
Ellison Onizuka, American astronaut

July 4
Ed O'Ross, American actor

July 9
Bon Scott, Australian rock singer of AC/DC
Mitch Mitchell, English drummer of The Jimi Hendrix Experience

July 16
Ron Yary, American football player

July 17
Alun Armstrong, English actor

July 25
Rita Marley, Jamaican singer

July 30
Neil Bonnett, American race car driver

August 1
Mike Emrick, American sportscaster
Sandi Griffiths, American singer

August 9
Jim Kiick, American football player

August 19
Charles Bolden, American astronaut

August 20
Ralf Hütter, German techno singer and musician of Kraftwerk

August 23
Keith Moon, English rock drummer of The Who

August 25
Charles Ghigna (Father Goose), American poet and children's author

August 26
Valerie Simpson, American singer
Mark Snow, American composer

September 2
Luis Avalos, Cuban-born American character actor
Billy Preston, American soul musician

September 9
Bruce Palmer, Canadian musician of Buffalo Springfield

September 10
Jim Hines, American athlete

September 11
Sandy Skoglund, American photographer

September 28
Jeffrey Jones, American actor

October 7
Catharine MacKinnon, American feminist

October 11
Daryl Hall, American rock musician of Hall & Oates

October 13
Demond Wilson, American actor and minister

October 14
Justin Hayward, English rock singer and songwriter of Moody Blues

October 15
Richard Carpenter, American musician and composer of The Carpenters

October 17
Bob Seagren, American athlete and actor

October 19
Philip Pullman, English author

October 27
Ivan Reitman, Slovakian-born film director and producer

October 31
Stephen Rea, Northern Irish actor

November 5
Gram Parsons, American musician

November 14
Carola Dunn, English writer

November 20
Alice Aycock, American sculptor
Greg Cook, American football player
Judy Woodruff, American television reporter

December 9
Sonia Gandhi, Indian politician

December 11
Susan Kyle aka Diana Palmer, American writer

December 16
Benny Andersson, Swedish rock singer and songwriter of ABBA

December 17
Eugene Levy, Canadian actor

December 19
Robert Urich, American actor

December 20
Dick Wolf, American television producer

December 21
Carl Wilson, American musician

December 23
Susan Lucci, American actress

December 25
Gene Lamont, American baseball player and manager

December 27
Janet Street-Porter, English broadcast journalist

December 29
Marianne Faithfull, English singer and actress

December 30
Patti Smith, American poet and singer

December 31
Diane von Fürstenberg, Belgian-American fashion designer

Facts and Figures of 1946

President of the U.S.
Harry S. Truman
Vice President of the U.S.
None (Truman was vice president and assumed the presidency after Franklin D. Roosevelt's sudden death in 1945)

Population of the U. S.
141,389,000
Births
3,411,000

High School Graduates
Males: 467,000
Females: 613,000

Average Salary for full-time employee:
$2,369.00
Minimum Wage (per hour): $0.40

Average cost for:

Bread (lb.)	$0.10
Bacon (lb.)	$0.53
Butter (lb.)	$0.71
Eggs (doz.)	$0.59
Milk (gal.)	$0.26
Potatoes (10 lbs.)	$0.47
Coffee (lb.)	$0.34
Sugar (5 lbs.)	$0.38
Gasoline (gal.)	$0.15
Movie Ticket	$0.35
Postage Stamp	$0.03
Car	$1,190.00
Single-family home	$7,100.00

Notable Inventions and Firsts

January 10: The U.S. Army Signal Corps begins Project Diana, bouncing radio signals off the moon and receiving the reflecting signals back on Earth. The Project launches the space age.

March 31: TWA begins the first service between the United States and Italy.

April 10: Women in Japan vote for the first time.

May: *The Common Sense Book of Baby and Child Care* by psychiatrist Benjamin Spock, 43, is published. The book's advice differs widely from what was commonly used for childrearing at the time.

July 5: Bikinis go on sale in Paris, but don't become popular in the United States until the 1960s.

August 1: Fulbright awards for international exchange study fellowships for students and professors are initiated when a bill introduced by Sen. J. William Fulbright is signed into law by President Truman.

October 1: Mensa, the self-proclaimed "high IQ society," is founded in the United Kingdom.

December 11: United Nations Children's Fund (UNICEF) is founded.

Sports Winners

NFL: Chicago Bears defeat New York Giants
World Series: St. Louis Cardinals defeat Boston Red Sox
Stanley Cup: Montreal Canadiens defeat Boston Bruins
The Masters: Herman Keiser wins
PGA Championship: Ben Hogan wins

Live It Again 1946

PROJECT EDITOR Richard Stenhouse
ASSISTANT EDITOR Erika Mann
ART DIRECTOR Brad Snow
COPYWRITER Jim Langham
MANAGING EDITOR Barb Sprunger
PRODUCTION ARTIST SUPERVISOR Erin Augsburger
PRODUCTION ARTISTS Erin Augsburger, Nicole Gage, Edith Teegarden
COPY EDITOR Amanda Scheerer
PHOTOGRAPHY SUPERVISOR Tammy Christian
NOSTALGIA EDITOR Ken Tate
COPY SUPERVISOR Michelle Beck
EDITORIAL DIRECTOR Jeanne Stauffer
PUBLISHING SERVICES DIRECTOR Brenda Gallmeyer

Printed in China
First Printing: 2010
Library of Congress Number: 2009904217
ISBN: 978-1-59635-276-6

Customer Service
LiveItAgain.com
(800) 829-5865

We would like to thank Curtis Publishing for the art prints used in this book. For fine-art prints and more information on the artists featured in *Live It Again 1946* contact Curtis Publishing, Indianapolis, IN 46202, (317) 633-2070, All rights reserved, www.curtispublishing.com

We would like to acknowledge and thank Phillips-Van Heusen Corporation, the owner of the ARROW trademark.

We would like to thank the Wisconsin Historical Society for the use of their online Photograph and Image collection (www.wisconsinhistory.org) and CNH America LLC.

We would like to acknowledge and thank the HMX Group, the owner of the Hart Schaffner Marx trademark.

1 2 3 4 5 6 7 8 9